I0098997

LIFT BRIDGE

Published by Lift Bridge Publishing
Copyright © 2014 by Sharee Harris
All Rights Reserved
Library of Congress Cataloging-in-Publication Data
Harris, Sharee.
I Fell in Love with Music
Book Cover artist: Sharee Harris
ISBN 978-0-692-35639-5
PRINTED IN THE UNITED STATES OF AMERICA
FIRST EDITION

Table of Contents

Words of Love

-Let me be
-Let me be the fire that burns for you. The one to call to be there for you. You had my body, now have my heart. I feel for you more than you know. I never felt this way about a person in my life. I have been in love but now I'm feeling so different. You make it that way. Hopefully you will never feel sadness when you think of me. You'll never hurt when you think of me. And when all else fails in your life there's just me. Two is the magic number. Just you and me. Hopefully things will only get better between us. Never a dull moment. (If you get what I mean)

Dedication

This is dedicated to you, you know who you are. I never knew I loved and hated you as much as I did. I never knew that I wrote so much about our beginning, middle and end. All I can say is thank you; you were my inspiration from the beginning. You brought out the best and worst of me. But life is a learning experience and this is mine. Through all the hurt and pain, I say thank you.
Forever in a Day

To my boys, you are truly gifts from God. I look at the both of you and I see my joy, peace and the true loves of my life. You were given to me and I am so grateful to be your mom. I am more than thankful for your lives. I love you more than words could every express.

Introduction

A Lyric of Poetry: "I Fell In Love with Music" is a book about a young woman who discovers that there is more in "love" than what the fairy tales say. This book explores her heart through a love she thought she would have for a lifetime. "I Fell In Love with Music", takes you on a roller coaster ride of feelings though love, hurt, joy, pain, romance and sex.

This book will give insight on the heart, spirit, soul and mind of a women in love, who has been broken hearted, and still finds joy in knowing love still exist.

My thoughts of being a mother

My joy, my life, my everything
The day God, brought you into
My life was a day of final
Peace, joy and happiness
You brighten up every part of me
When I am down
Your smile completes me
Your soul makes me whole
Even though things are not
The way I want them to be
Just between you and me
We will make it through all
Odds, good and bad
I thank God and your father
Every day for you
You make me so happy
When you cry and all I have to do
Is kiss your lips and you stop
You are my baby Noah
And whatever you want
Or need I will be
There to get it for you
You shell never want for nothing
You are more precious than life
And I am grateful that you let me be your mom
The love of my life
The joy that brightens up everything May God bless you and keep
you safe

Chapter 1
Relating all to life, love and pain…

My life is like a movie and I don't know what the outcome will be.

Brown Sugar is the movie that relates to where I am and where I want to be. See there is so much more to me then what meets the eye. There are so many things that have happen in my life that has placed me where I am today. But love has me here, has me at this moment. Love has me on the edge of losing everything that I have worked so hard for.

See the story is about a year from this date, well a year from the date I first started writing this book. I fell in love with this guy that at one point in our lives, we were best friends. We were happy and all of sudden at a moment in a church parking lot change the game between us. We took things to another level. Another level that made my world feel so complete. He made me happy; he made everything in me feel like I was on cloud nine. Our love was unreal. He was my peacemaker, my joy and my life. The greatest lover I ever had but things changed, I don't know how or why. But things changed and we are no longer together.

A movie, I'm placed back there and looking at it all "She fell in love with hip-hop";" I fell in love with music". Such a beautiful soul and spirit very talented and anointed beyond belief but drama pledged and I find myself lost in music. Trying to find the tune to this song that sounds like someone is breaking glass over and over again. The music isn't right, it's painful and in a deep dream that you cannot get out of.

Music, the love of my life a passion so great. But a memory…

Chapter one is all of poems that come from a relationship in its prime. Relating life, love and pain is what chapter one is all about.

You

I don't know what this is
My heart is so full
Each poem I write is inspired by a man
This man is you
At this moment I am happy
Not sad or depressed but happy
It's funny how a man can change so much
Just by his presences and love for you
Even though right now the timing is wrong for him
But perfect for me
I just don't know what this is
As Jay-Z is ringing in the background
With each beat of this song
And the bass of each ooooh....
I am thinking of you
What is this?
Is this list or love?
It's been about I guess 5-7 years since we have known
Each other
But only now we will
AND
Shall explore a territory of unknown
We will explore a ground
That we both know should be left alone
But can't because this is the only chance we get
This game we play is like a boomerang
It has disappeared and came back
But the next time
It may not come back
They say if it is meant to be then it will be
And

Continue....

Two love birds can sing
See that boomerang is here
And doesn't want to be let go
But hold it tight, just hold it
Hold it tight
And in time
You shall
See what
Time shall tell

Special

My thoughts of you
A special yet sweet
Undying thoughts of you
You have brighten my world
Showed me what love is
Mr. Wonderful is your name
We praise you
The most unspeakable joy of my life
You shell walk in a great path
And love like no other

Thought of You Today

I thought of you today
You were on my mind
And my insides start to melt
It's something that you do
When you walk in a room
That turns my emotions and
My body upside down
I get shaky
When you touch me
I feel like I want to
Take that extra step
With you
But then I pull away and take my time
So that things won't end up
Like my past relationship
I look at you and I see me
Exploring your innermost
Thoughts
And your presences
I can't control myself
You are all I want and need
I'm confused
My body in need
But I wait
Until I get a ring
I wait until you appear
I wait until…

Thank you

Thank you
Thank you
For the gift you have given me
December 7, 2001 was the day
Noah De'Juan Sellman
Was conceived
In the beginning it was a joy
So undefined
But now it's the greatest gift anyone could have
Ever given me
I thank you
For the night
And I thank you
For my gift
Something that she'll always
Be in debt to you for
Thank you not once but twice
For giving me the love
Of my life

Before you

Before you there was just me
Getting myself together with school
Hanging out with my friends
Getting over a failed attempt at a relationship
Before you
I was at peace
Not worrying about having a man
Even being with one
In a month and a half
I have cried more tears
Shattered my heart about a thousand times
Made an ass out of myself
Spent more money
And just plan acted like an fool
Before you
I was happy and sometimes sad
Before you
I was lonely but that was something I would live with
Before you
I never felt hate like I do right now
I can't explain why you called me
You can't explain why you just can't let go
And I in return cannot explain the actions that I
Am going to take
I can't explain why my heart hurts and the one thing
I should do
I can't because I want you so bad
Before you
There was me
Alone, sad and happy
Before you

Continue....

I was at least sane
Before you
There was just me

You

What do we do now?
Pledged with so much
On a mind
So very lost
But a heart so heavy
It's another Sunday
And we must thank God for
That
And for our lives as they are
My morning prayer
I ask for forgiveness
And I shall receive it
My morning prayer
To you
Keep God always
And the thoughts of
Your trouble mind will
Soon come to pass

The back of your mind

I cannot speak
You know my mind and my heart better than I do
You understand my feelings and my thoughts
But I just don't know what your intensions are
I don't know whether to be scared, confused or if I should
Scream
I love you one minute then hate you the next
It hurts so bad because you are what I want
I don't want to say good-bye
I don't want to let go
I can't find the words to say what I want
What do I do?
You ask God to help you find away
But what I want is for you to find your way
God gives you choices and they are always in two's
But it is up to you and only you to make your own discussion
Your life is planned out already for you
Two different life plans
I keep saying I understand
But I don't
She has your thoughts, mind, your body, soul, spirit and interest
And most of all she has you
It works both ways
At this moment you have all of her in you
And I cannot fight that
I don't know what to think or believe
I feel as though I don't know
How you feel about me
It's crazy because I am all you want and all you need
But there is something between us
Something that should not be

Continue....

But it is
Just follow your heart
Don't give into crazy interest
Just love me the way you want
Give me a chance to breath
Deep within your soul
Let me express the way I feel
Don't push me away
Even though you may think you're not
I don't want to write another poem
I don't want to sing another sad love song
I just want you to understand my heart
And for me to trust and understand yours
I'm scared and I just don't know what to do
Just help me
Help me
Release the thoughts from the back of your mind

Friends

It's funny how I hear a quote from a wise man
And
It gets me to think of the friends in my life
I can remember the day I met you
You wanted to fight me over some beef you had with this little child
Then there's the other friend who I all of sudden have because of a man she let go off
I can't stand shady ass people and the thoughts that they may have in their head
Just to get what they want
Don't pretend that you care about me and the things that I am doing with myself
Don't place my name in your mouth with some type of plan behind it
I don't need you in my life as a friend
I don't need the drama that you plan to bring this way
I don't need the comments
I don't need you in my business
I don't need the looks or the remarks
What I need is for you to let me breathe and enjoy the situation that I am in
A situation that you obviously don't want me in
See right now I have something that you want
You want your click back and all the fun things that all may have done
But see there is this chick that has destroyed that for you
And
Now and only now you need something to do
Your life is so empty because you lost a soul that held everything together
Your bored and needed a life but I don't want you in mine

Continue....

I have too many friends that I can handle
And
Therefore I do not need you
Being shady is not the game of the future
Just let it go
Let me keep what I have
Get a life and move on
No more new friends

Another

Love is love
Love has no bearing
No direction
It's just love
Sometimes it's hard to accept all things
That goes with love
Whether good or bad
Love is crazy
And it pulls you in all directions
But once you're in love
You have to learn how to let go
And let nature take its course
Because what's meant to be will be
In love you need to realize
What the other is saying and just take it for what's it worth
Friends is all you want us to be
So a friend I shall be
Not a lover but a friend
The madness will stop
And your life you can live
Love
What a word
With such power
It makes the strongest person weak
The battle of a broken heart
Only wanting one thing
But this is the time to be patient
And what they say, be still
Because in our heart of hearts
What you have with another
Is not real

Continue....

Because if so this game we
Would not be play
Love and sex
Sex the biggest sin of all
And to find you're true
Thoughts and direction
You want to be in
The sex will stop
It has to stop
Love
Look where it has placed us
Back to where we started
In time
The essence of all of this
Will be revealed
And your heart will be true
And true love you shell have
Love isn't it funny

Free

I feel like a bird flying in the sky
Without a care in the world
I feel like a lion roaring in the wild
I feel like a monkey climbing the trees
I just feel so free
So free to be me
Free to love
Free to express myself to the world
Free to let go of the past and just move
On and feel so free
That I don't feel like me
I just feel so free
Like a plane in the sky
I feel so free

Like Mike

Everyone wants to be like Mike
Wants to know his every move
His every thought
But Mike doesn't understand why
If you feel like
You have all you want
And what you have
Is just right
Then why watch
Every move Mike makes
Why do you want to know about?
Mike
Worry about yourself
And handle your own
Affairs
Before you get your feelings hurt
Mike likes all
But hates the ones
That say they are one way
But act so differently
Don't hate on Mike
Love Mike
Come out with it
Because Mike is listening
But don't cross the line
Because you will get
Hurt
Everybody wants to be like MIKE

Today

Today is the day that the Lord has made
And more than anything I am glad in it
The essence of today
The beauty of tomorrow
And just the growth of my life
Makes me happy
It's just today
And the rest of my life
Has just placed
Me here today
Happy

The Calmness of a Woman

You ask me how I keep my cool
I respond
I was placed here for a reason
I was given to you as a gift
As a friend
And then later as a lover
You want me to break my cool
Release some anger
Throw a brick
Even scream to the no man lands
But I can't
That's just the calmness of a woman
God does not put more on us
Then we cannot bear
He gives us hope, joy and a lighted tunnel
He places them to you in all shapes, sizes, faces and creatures
In this presence of an essence
You have me
The calmness of a Queen

Relationships

Almost a half a decade you were with someone
And out of the blue she let you go
You take some time to mend a broken heart
But then in turn you place someone else in your life
To cover up the hurt and pain
You place someone in your life, to play the field
Knowing all the time that this was nothing but a game
See you have one player, one on base and the other
Is up to bat
Three strikes and player number two is out the game
And player number one wins
See to you this game is only fair
Because it's hard for you
To face the big mess that you have made
You're so afraid to move on
Because of what if questions
And the fact that you still love her
But you fail to realize that life is all about
Break ups and new relationships
Life is about exploring what's out there without
Even looking back
I look at it this way I was never in the running
Just on the sidelines
To bring you true love home to you
That's ok though
Life is also about obstacles and the price
You pay
And this is just mine

Mr. Wonderful

Do I make you mad or happy?
Do I please you?
Do you think you would or could see yourself with me for life?
Do your feelings change when you leave my house?
And you go into a different mindset and you go
And do the same thing to me to her
Do you think of me?
Would you cry for me?
Would you fight for me?
Would you place a ring on my finger and say this is forever
Are you willing to take a chance and just move on?
Would you move the earth to make me happy?
Would you move the sun so that I would have shade?
Would you love me?
The answer is yes and that's why you are Mr. Wonderful

Haters

Don't take away my shine
Don't hate me for what I do
Don't look at me and ask
What can I do to blow her shine?
I have had enough
I have had enough
Of you and all your people
Stay away from me
Don't trace tales to me
Don't make me feel the way you do
Be your own person
And move on like me
Let the asshole be an asshole
Because all things come to light
And soon and real soon
That light will shine
Don't hate me for something
You created
Love me
For taking over something that's
Not worth dirt
Don't hate me
But move on
And leave me alone

Confused

There is not a day that goes by that I do not ask myself
Why is love so confusing or just why the process
Of being with someone so confusing
There is not a day that goes by when I ask myself
Should I just concentrate on school and put men to aside until I
have my career
Or
Should I just take what God has placed in front of me and run
with it
I am so confused
I cry at night because everything I want, I have placed in front of
me but is at a
Distance that I cannot grip
It's like I have the plan all figure out and then all of a sudden
I am thrown a curve ball
That's why I am so confused
Through being confused I do know what I want
And I don't plan to let go

Baby

Just a touch across my stomach the sweet innovation of the thought
from a man
Saying I can see you having my baby
Gives me the thought of motherhood
How it would be to be a mother and how my life would change
I wonder sometimes if my child would grow up like one
Fatherless
Or would my child have a loving father
That will be there for him/her throughout his/her life
I think about the smell, the look, the weight, and the smile of my
baby
I think about nine months of pregnancy
I look at the delivery and how scared I would be
I think of the father and if he will be there or not
Where is all of this coming from?
Is it that I am reaching out for something that is not there?
Like the love of a father
The love of a man
I wonder what a baby would do to my life
I wonder about love
I wonder if
Baby

Chapter Two
After it all, the drama of a broken heart

In a moment, he broke my heart. That's why we are here. In a moment I felt so lost and hurt. I never felt so much pain before in my life. Not understanding the things that have happen between us. He walked away without a shadow of a doubt and left me pregnant and heart broken.

The series of tears and the emotions of being alone is what chapter two is all about!

I can't go back in time when we were happy and not sad. When we could talk and share it all. But now we don't talk, can't talk and we are blinded by what if and maybes. Drama of a broken heart is what's next and what's there to come.

From the beginning of time, women have been the ones to fall so deep in love with a man. And sometimes that man doesn't love you all the same, the day that all is revealed; your heart can't take it. Because what you thought you had, you really didn't have at all.

Brokenness can teach you so many lessons about life and can lead you into a destiny you never knew you had. Brokenness is the journey God gave me so that I can heal and appreciate what life has to offer. In life we all have to go through something and "Brokenness" was what I had to go through to get what God has for me. Don't be a shame of hurt and pain because it can bring so much joy when you're healed.

Pain/Foolish

I have played the fool for too
Long
And it's time to move on
My heart and my eyes cannot take anymore
Here I have a child
In my womb
That places so much meaning on my
Life
And all I do is sit and
Worry about you
The one that cause me all this pain
The one that can't tell the truth
If it hit him in his face
I am tired
I'm sick
I have all this love for a man
That doesn't feel the same way
His mind is plague by another
That gives him no stress and no drama
His mind is plague by the fact that
She is fresh and ready to be open
Plague by the fact that he can start over
And this time do it right
Plagued by what he thinks is the
Perfect person for him
So blinded by the di in his pants
He can't see
The hurt and pain he has caused
All the sleepless nights
And the wet pillows
It's time for that to be over

Continue....

Because he doesn't want YOU
He wants another
It's time to get a grip
Of all the times you were pass
By
And still are
Time to tell myself that
I am one in million
And anyone who has me is the lucky
One
I have done all that I can
I have said all that I can say
I have cried my last tear
I have made this the last time I will make a fool out of myself
It's a shame
I have never done anything to hurt
You
But in return I am filled with so much pain and hurt
I can't walk away that easy
But I refuse to be around much longer
If I had a penny for every tear
I would be rich off your love alone
But instead I have nothing
But a broken heart and a lot
Of what if questions
I don't hold the cards in my hand
For the future
But I hold my destiny right beside
Me
And maybe one day this will
Be a faded dream
A soap opera to tell our kids
Maybe hand and hand we will be in a
Church confessing what went wrong and
What went right to bring us together?

Continue....

We never had the right timing for Love
But God must see different
Because we will never be apart
As we know this is one of life's journeys we must take to finally
get love right
You had 4 1/2 years and a 5 month Romance
I had months and a 5 month romance
And it just never worked
So maybe this is to prepare us for
The reunion of two souls
No one will ever replace what we had
And will have
It's just all in time
That together again we will be
A matter of time that you will see me gone
See that I have moved on and
Will no longer be waiting for you
I have said my peace and the possible vision of tomorrow
But I will not be foolish anymore
Love is Love
And moving on is a must
So let two ships be passed by this one time and see if they Shell
ever sail by one another again
Because life is too short to
Hold on to something that's not there
It's time to stop being FOOLISH...

Rain Drops

I love you with all my heart
With every tear
With every song
I can remember love
Especially when it was good love
Last night you made
Love to me
Like no other
You spoke to me in a language of body talk
Your mouth
Your hands
Your body on mines
I knew this moment was going
To come and I knew that this
Would be the last moment
That we would share
You placed another part of
Yourself inside me
You gave me a hope
But then the reality of it all
Came into play
And then I finally see
What's out there for me?
And right now that's not you
On the real there is no other
In my life right now
But in all fairness
I need to stop what I am doing
And move on
Each tear I cry
Shows me more and more each day

Continue....

What it is I need to do
There was always you
Always love for you
My heart you will never know
My body you have explored
But you will never leave another for me
All we can do is walk away
And be parents only to a
Young boy who needs
Our guidance and love
You do what you do
And I shell do what I do
But this time apart
That's the way you made it
Pictures speak to me and I have seen enough
Tears
Tears
Tears
That's all that's left
And we are a distant memory
That will always be

Picture This

Picture this
Me not there
But at a distance that
You cannot reach
Picture this
My heart belonging
To another
I wonder if you would care
I wonder if the tears I cry
Are in vain
Where is all of this going?
Is there a second chance
For love
Picture this
Me walking away
As I am now
Picture this
The chains are locking
Around my heart
Picture me
A faded memory
Of what you once had
Words there are so many
And at times they block
The mind of what needs
To be said
To many words
So little time
Picture this
Picture me
Gone

One Drawn Out Mess
The Finally

In a drop of an eye
My world changed
Lost dreams, hopes and love
My world was torn
And my heart was broken
A baby we have created
Together
Has to sit and watch
A world so cold
And parents that can't get along
There's a room full of lost desires
There's a place where my child is
That has to live the life
His mom doesn't want him to
Desperate measures
Places me back to square one
None of this I want
None of this I can bare
My life
You started something
You can't finish
It started with words
In a church parking lot
The word "HI" was enough
You caught my eye
A phone call I receive
With a date in mind
You enter my life
Heartbroken with thoughts

Continue....

Of a past love
A love you loved for four years
But you left that there
And love you gave me
A date, a trip, a moment
That gave us a relationship out the ordinary
In less than a years' time
We saw the world
We enjoyed each other
In spite of all the drama and the pain
But in one split second you
Tore all we had apart
For a love you cannot be true to
You placed yourself in another life
Giving her you're all
Taking the things we did
And then doing them with her
Nothing is different that you share
Nothing but this story is repeating itself
A pattern you have created
My pictures you have replaced
And a heart you have destroyed
Wanting you
Needing you
Feeling like I can't live without you
What have you done to me?
How can my love be so deep?
And yours just gone

Battle

My battle I have to
Fight alone
The battle of a broken heart
That only seems to keep getting
Wounded instead of being healed
I feel like I am going to in up
In a mental institution
Because my heart is so heavy
And my tears are so loud
With every drop of each tear
I can remember all the things
You did to me to hurt me
With each drop all I see is
Your face and all the hurt
And pain
And the question
Comes in my head
What did I do to you?
For you to do this to me
You reply nothing
But why do I stand here alone
Why is it that you have moved on
And I am stuck with a broken heart
I look at you and feel HATE
I don't deserve this
I never asked for this
Why me
With each day it gets harder
With each moment
I feel more lost
You where the love of my life

Continue....

And now you are my enemy within
I'm fighting a battle
A battle I can't seem to win
I cannot find a way out
Because you will be in my
Life forever
Because of a child we share
No one has ever treated me as you
Have
And in a moment pass
No one ever will
This is my BATTLE

Tears

I have so many tears falling down my face
And I just don't know why
My heart is beating so fast
The tears start from a women yelling at me
I just don't understand life anymore
From family to old friends
My life seems so crazy
I'm not in school, I don't work
All I do is sleep
And that's not me
I want to get out and enjoy life
And stop dreaming of a downfall
Of the love of my life
I'm scared that all my thoughts
Are going to become true
My heart is heavy
Because I put so much on it
I need to stop living for the past
And just start living for today
Go out and do things by myself
It shouldn't be that hard
It's just the fact that I am so use of getting
What I want
And not use to it disappearing

Happy

I want to be happy
But I feel sad without you
But that is over
I have come to my senses
When it comes to you
You have proved all but so many
Times that you are not worthy any of
My time
Or
My body
You put a spell
On me
And now the spell has been broken
All I had to do was open my eyes
And see you for you
I have been played for a fool
And sad over you
I want to be happy
And looking at you makes
Me unhappy
So happy I shall be
But happy I will be
Without you

Thoughts

I never knew I had so much love inside me
But I do
I never knew love would be like this
I wrapped a part of my life in someone who really
Didn't care for me
The way I cared for him
He never keeps my picture on his keys
Never keep my pictures up
They were always forced
My body wants him
And my heart hurts
Maybe one day soon this will be over
And my love for him will go away
Just my thoughts

Love

I was in love
Once before
I know I was
I know it wasn't anything
I know there was a lot more
To the love I had then what
Meets the eye
I was in love
Once before
I know I was
But it seems so long ago
Even though the love was just here
I was in love
I know I was
But what about you
If you ever loved me
The way you said you did
Then you would have never hurt me the
Way you do
You took what I had and
Throw it all away
And now I must move on
I was in love
Once before
I know I was
But I woke up one
Day and it was all gone
I know I was in love

It's over, the end of Us

It's over
My heart cannot take anymore
That door is finally closed
And it shell never be opened again
It's over
No more US
No more making love
No more long night phone calls
No more anything
Everything about us is through
The end to a long journey
Has no hope of a new beginning
My heart aches and I shell feel
Pain and a lost for a time to come
Love is special
But there always has to be an
End to a beginning
My love shell never die
But it's over
The final ferry of the end
You were my baby
My love, my life
But it's over
Forever in a day

Emotions

A once in a lifetime thing
A once in a lifetime hurt and pain
I will only go through this one time
And any other love shell be
One in a million
My first love
The one I would have done
My all for
Has left me for another
And it's too late to turn back
I am like an emotional roller coaster
Lost and confused
Trying to fight my heart
Trying to walk away from a
Man I love so deeply
Relationships are special
And I want is an old love back
But what shell I do
Emotions

Questions

Wait a minute
Don't go to sleep
Tell me how you feel
Don't walk away
Come back and listen to your heart
Do you love me or are you in love with me
Do you urine for me when I am not there
Do you think of me?
Is your body full of deep emotions?
That you can only express
When our lips and body become one
What is this are you afraid of me
Why did you go away?
Why run to another
Is it because I have more
Of an responsibility to bare
And she doesn't
Why say what you say
Do we want the same thing?
Or are we on two different paths
Too many questions
Very little answers
The meaning of love shell
Define all
And every question
Shell be answered

You Part II

Once again that boomerang
Has been let go
It has disappeared and there's
No telling if it will come back
We have explored no man's land
And have felt a lot of pain and hurt from it
I look into your eyes and I see
All things that I want out of life
But what you may always want is
Not good for you
You have opened my heart to
So much
But now it's time to move on
I don't know what this is
My heart is so heavy
Each poem I write is inspired by you
You
It took 7 years for us to get here
And only 8 months for us to part
We were once two love birds
But now there's one
That boomerang is gone
And what's meant to be will be
The love I have shell always be
But me
I will not be
Just a faded memory
Of all
The good and bad times we share
You are you
The one that she'll always be
But without me
By your side

Men

My first big break up
From the day of my break up
I have had a lot of men
That wanted to talk to me
But none of them were
Ever true
Not true to me
Nor themselves
I have lied and played games
That a child would play
I fight with the thought of men
Wondering why
They don't want me
But only want me for what I can do for them
They all walk away from me
They leave
With no reason
And I'm left feeling
The pain and emptiness of my lost soul
I ache
I cry
I don't know what to do
Men
What have I done?
That makes them all go away
I chose to look at
God to find my way
But I still feel loss
Because I'm truly not there
I'm not in God's grace like should be
So until then
I will be lost

Continue....

Sad and confused
In spite of what I want
The only man I need to accept
In my life is God and God alone
He will be the father that left, the boyfriend I lost
The husband I shell have and a provider
For my son
Men
And the ups and downs
That's the story of my life

Confessions

True confession of my soul
True confession of my first love
A first love that speaks to me from a far
A true love were there are no words but just
Thoughts
My first love will always be with me
Near me and inside me
I never had a first love
I always thought things would be different
But I would not ask for it to be any other way
All the pain and the heartaches
The lonely nights
The thoughts of a cheating soul
A soul crying and confused
I wouldn't trade it in for nothing in the world
A hard fought battle
That had to end
Makes me cry
Because my first love
I will all ways want
My selfishness, my emptiness, my mind and my mouth
Tore us apart
But what no man can put us under
God can bring back together
If it's meant to be
My first love
I will always love
My first love
Such a spirited soul
My first love
That I shell love forever

Thoughts Part II

I know why I do the things I do
Now
I don't call
Because you are never there
My thoughts are so heavy
Because of the way I feel right now
I spoke my mind and said my peace
But I want you so bad right now
I want the full package of sex/ lovemaking
I want foreplay
A game or two
I want love
And just to have my body
Played with
I want you
But you are nowhere to found
I don't want a 2:00 a.m. phone call
From you
I want to speak to you now
This makes me sick
The way I feel and just all the things
I want, I never get
I'm going crazy
Just thinking of everything
Do you think of me?
Like I think of you
Do wonder or ever had the thought of us being one again
Are you pledged by decisions?
That blows your mind
Tell me
What

Continue....

Why is my life such a mess?
Why do I want you so bad?
Right now you are with another
And I am sad
And wish you were here
I'm going to cry
So this is the end

Time

Time waits for nothing
And in time all wounds
Will heal
In time
Life shall get better
Life won't be as difficult
As they have been
In time
I won't regret the
Decisions I made as far as
Love goes
Let me take a minute
And let a poetic of love flow
My life is full of time
Patients and in the inquiry of love
See I once was in love
With a man
But our two worlds
Are not meeting
And while one wants the other
The other has a new love
And the other can't handle that
See in time poetic
This speaker of a poetic mind, body and spirit
Thinks only of love lost
She wants so much
That in time she shell receive
It's painful to move on
From a love that you
Thought would be yours forever
Questions pledged her

Continue....

And poetic sits back and waits
And see what life has for her
I wonder if he thinks of me
Does his mind get twisted?
When I walk in a room
Does he say damn she looks good?
Can I have her?
In time I wonder if poeticallywet thinks or ask the question will
we ever be together again
Does he want that or if
He had the thought of love
This love being a part of his life
Time
Time
Life is short
And time waits for nothing
And poetic the essence of love
Will be gone
Her dark days and lonely nights
Will be taken care of by another
And in time
Her broken heart will heal
And love will enter again
But only when the time is right

Confession of a Blown Mind

My love runs deeper than an ocean
My love shows from day to day
I feel so much heart ache and pain
When all I want is love
I feel your body on mines
When you are away
I love your smell and touch
I love the way you hold me
But I messed things up
Because of my mouth and always wanting to do things
But now there's a new love
That is a vision of me
Every part of what she is and does
All I see is me
The man I love has moved on
And I have to accept the fact
Of just being friends
Right now he has everything
He wants and needs
From an arrangement that I know he loves
No one can take away the pain
No one can take away the hurt
No one can take away the love
That I have for this man
All I ask is for another chance
Another chance at love with him
Another chance to explore the world
 With him and
Through his eyes see the world
I feel like I'm starting over
And

Continue....

Fighting to win a winless battle
The other women knows how to play the game
She knows what to say and what to do to make things right
She knows how to play the hand
She has been dealt
And
I might say very well
She's not going to leave one rock unturned
Get in good with the baby mommy
So then get in good with the baby
And then get the prize to be won
She knows how to mend a broken heart
And all I do is cause it more pain
It's like the duel of the friends
Be a friend to him/go out with him
We both are in the same boat
As far as being this man friend
It's like a test to see
Who does it better and how it can be done
It's on
Let the battle begin
Because I'm not about to give up on the love of my life
Outside of what outsiders may say or think
A friend I will be
But a fool I will not
It's the battle of the innocent
And the battle is on

The Awakening

You have come back into my life
Awakening a restless soul
Showing love, warmth, peace and joy
All the things I let slip away when you left
You have come back into my life
Like a raft going down a spiral stream out of control
You have awaken my body, my soul, my mind, my everything
To just destroy it once again
You left I cried
You left I wept
You left and I destroyed me
Now you're back and leaving again
But instead of pain and sorrow
This awakening soul wants revenge
From busting the windows out your car
To accidentally letting my foot off the brake pedal as you stand in
front my car
You have come back into my life
Only to walk out again
So instead of enduring pain, instead of giving into revenge
I let go and let God, not to let you in my life again
No man should awaken a soul without the intend of loving her
So walk slowing, no faster
Before this awaken soul awakes you

Chapter 3

SEX

My first is what he was. He turned me out and showed me things that I never knew before. Sex is what you make it. But don't let it make you. We have done it all when it came to sex. We have experienced it all, different places, different objects... If you can think about it we did it.

So enjoy the details of non-lonely night.

Addictive

Why are you trying to fight?
What is the problem?
You have enter the world of me
And cannot leave
Damn I must have put something
On ya
Smile
It's the fashion of me
The one that makes your dreams come true
You have entered me
The home wrecker
It's funny
Because my thoughts are in order
By the challenge of a loss
Cause
Addictive
That's what I am

A vision of you

I had a dream last night
That in vision me and you
And
We were not wearing anything standing real close to each
Other dancing to a Luther Vandross song
There was no loving making in
The Sense of physical
But
In the sense of emotional
Power and just a great presence of two souls becoming one
The mood was so right
As you went to explore what I had in my inner thoughts
My inner body and my soul
The kisses you placed on me were so calm and very passionate
With your breath on my sweaty back and your tongue on my
shoulder
I start to get chills
And then you lay me down on my side of the bed
Place a sheet over me
Blow out the candles and turn off the lights
You start to move close to me
And you start to explore me for me
As you lay next to me with one arm on my stomach and the other
holding me tight all
Through the night until
The Alarm rings and then we must
Awake from a fantasy gone so right!

Last Night

The movement of my body and the swaying of my hips
Puts me in a mood that you cannot believe
My body, your body, and everything in between is good together
You place your hands on my hips
You place your lips on my breast
You hold me
But we never cross that line of intercourse
But some of the most passionate moments are the ones you don't expect
My body feels like it was made love to
My heart explodes with the caress of your tongue on my back
You're afraid you may get attached
But have you ever thought that you may already be attached
When two birds connect they sing
When two hearts are confused
It leads to last night
I can't explain why my body wants you so much
I don't know if it is to prove a point
Or
Just to show you how much I care
You asked about the L word
And I reply I feel as though some moments I feel like I just need to say I love you
But can't because we are not there yet
It's crazy how last night sparked up so much
Its funny how there is two people so crazy about each other
But there is still a wall between the two
Last night was so powerful
But the next night will be wonderful
When you take me, hold me, caress me, and make love to me
The next night when two souls become one

Continue....

Will complete such a beautiful last night that two souls are still one
We are more connect then you think
And that's last night

My Oh My

My Oh My
My oh my
The expression on your face
When you woke this morning
Turning over and only seeing
A rose on the pillow
And a note
That says I love you
Have a good day
You roll over with a big smile
Wanting me there to be there
With you
Not knowing that I am there
Standing in the mist watching you waiting for you to make your
first move
Of the day
Damn
I look at you and
See my life
I see my future in you
A good man
Not about games
But about love

Original Sin

A life of pain and misery
The original sin
The sins of all sins
Sex
I can't walk away
With a heart so heavy
The original sin
The life I live
Is pledged by the death of my
Opening legs that wants
More and desires more
Every time I see his round face
A moment in the back seat of a
Hyundai elantra
You hitting me from the back
As I roll my hips around
While you're inside me
Making me wet all over
With the sweat off your body
All over mine
My hair-dripping wet
With each impulse of our lovemaking
No not sex
But lovemaking
Just walking away
From hearing a word
A word of God's word
And I revoke and say I won't sin
But your lips turn me on
And I am back in your arms again
You say in the middle of lovemaking

Continue....

We need to stop
But we still continue as you rise
And as I peak
Playboy is what I call your di
As it works me inside out
We won't stop
There's too much that keeps us together
I have sinned
The original sin of the father
I ask you
Wanting you
Needing you to crave my appetite
You need me
You want me
And together we
Posse the original life of sin

Out of Control

My body is going out of control
Demanding your presence
But you're not here
My body is going out of control
With the passion and desire to be wrapped in your arms
But you're not here
My body feels like a glass window being hit by a bat
The wetness flows just as the glass shatters
But you're not here
My body, my hips, my hands, my heart wrenching feeling of you
in me
But you're not here
The door opens
Panties drop, phone falls, thrown up against the wall
As I take your clothes off, placing every part of your male anatomy
in my mouth
Now we both are out of control
As one leg is raised on the counter top, your head in between my
legs
Making every part of my body scream
With a flip of bending me now over the counter top
You place your big black penis inside one of the most amazing
holes I have on my body
Hair pull, juices flowing, sweat dripping, loud yelling
But it doesn't stop there the counter isn't enough and no one wants
to explode yet
With only black red bottoms on, I lead you to the stairs
As foreplay commence
Floor boards are broken
After coming in your mouth, you slide it in
You moan "damn baby this is good"

Continue....

Three minutes later you pull out and in my mouth in goes
You're cum dripping all down my mouth
Until the next episode
My body, your body all out of control

Overrated

They say sex is overrated
I say sex is good
Just that warm touch of a man
Just his caress
Sex is what you make it
And what it becomes of you
People worry so much now and days
That it's spooky
You cannot overrate a word
That most people know nothing about
Don't take advantage of something that can
Destroy your life
Enjoy when the time is right
Wait until you're ready to handle it
And love the one you are with
Before you take it too far
That's SEX

Sex

Sex
The pleasure of
Something so real
The way a man
Can work what he has
That can make
Every desire and dream
Of ecstasy come true
Sex
A night of passion
That turns into
Something unreal
With the lick from
A tongue that's placed
On your back
The lips that are placed
On your other lips
The movement all
So right
Making everything wet
You place your mouth
On his di
Making every part of oral
Sex so pleasure
That in an impulse
His toes curl up
The leg starts to shake
But before it goes too far
You pull away
And you start to dance
Taking off the rest of your clothes

Continue....

Like a stripper would
But you pause again
And tease him some more
Then you place yourself
On him
Making him say words
That he never spoke before
Playing with his ear
And his neck
Rolling yourself around
Going up and down
Then changing positions
About three to four times
Before you and him
Reach your climax
Together
But the fun doesn't stop
There
To be cont'd...

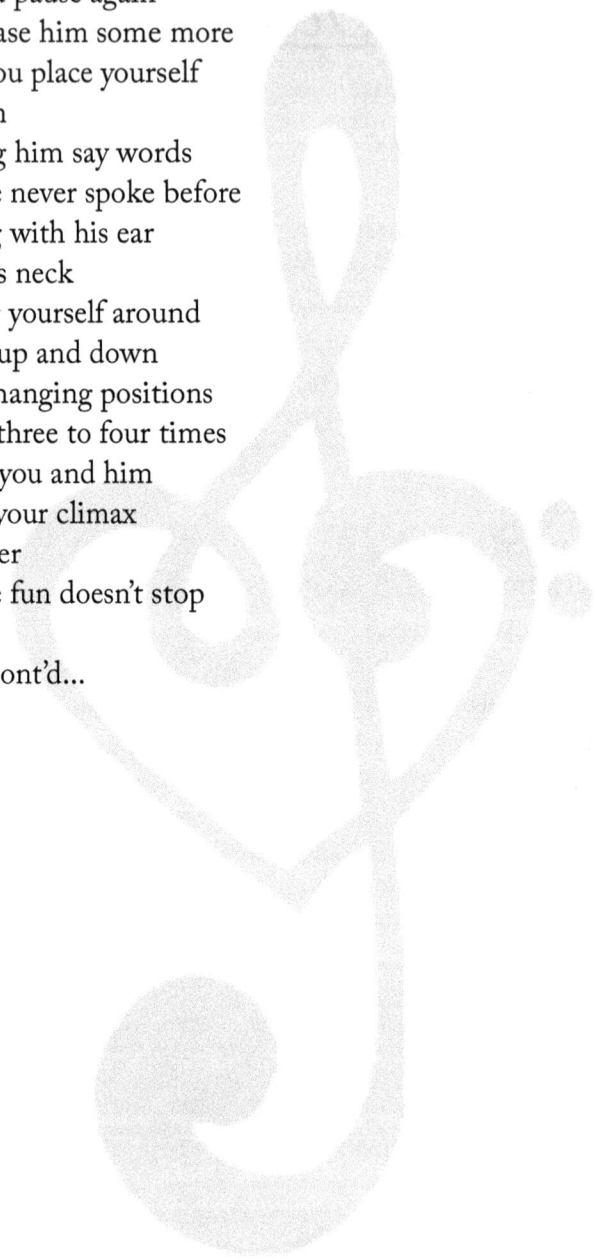

The Other Women

How did I get here?
Why did you put me here?
Why break up with me
And then won't leave me alone
Addictive is what I am
The sex is so good
That you can't walk away
Won't walk away
And don't have attentions
On doing so
A girlfriend you have
So blinded by what she
Thinks she got
When we both have the same thing
I'm the other women
The one that satisfy
Every thought you have
I am the essence of
Love making
That you won't leave
Tell me something
How long will this go
On
You say you're so in love
With one
But continue to break
Two hearts
You discuss me
You make me sick
So blinded by the
Di you have

Continue....

You can't see straight
Promises you break
And a loser you have
Become
But the other women
I continue to be
Not wanting to let go
But wanting to move on
This is the tale of
The other women
To be cont'd

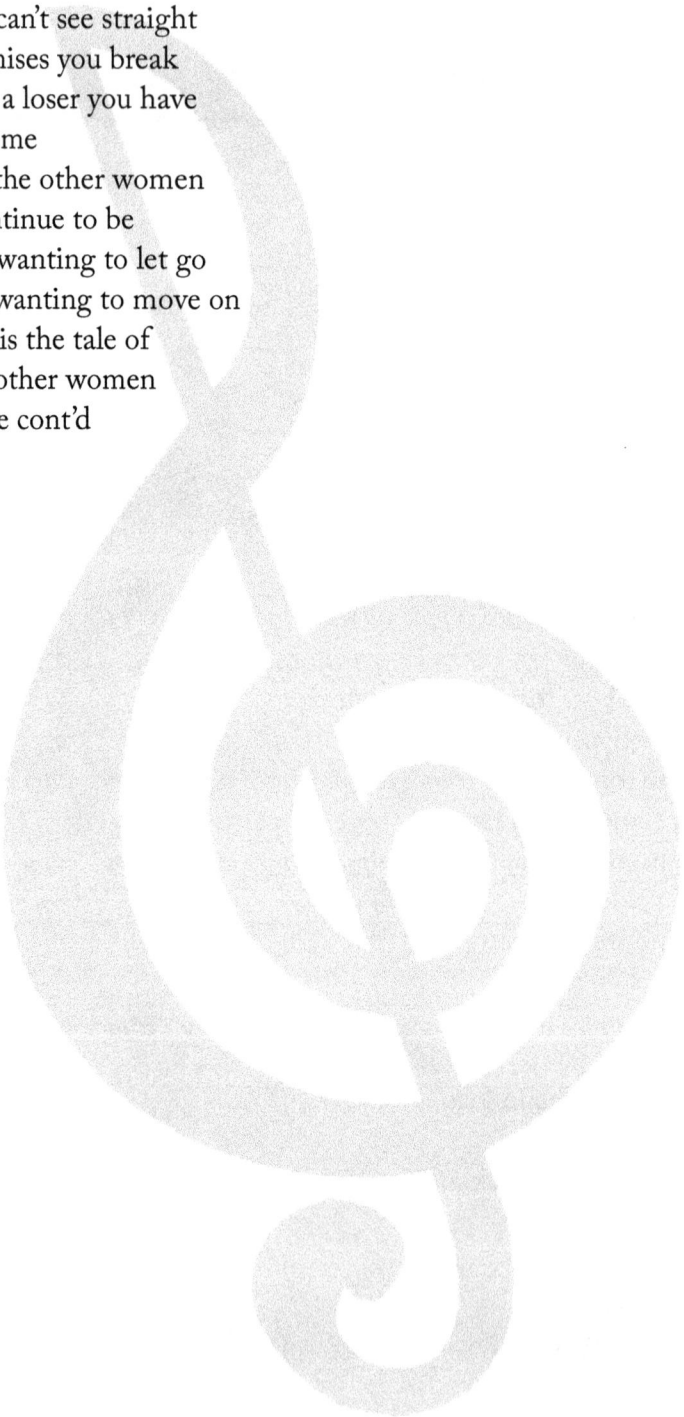

My Body

I never knew I could move my hips that way
Or
I never knew I was so comfortable with my body
That I could move to a beat to satisfy my man
I never knew my body could speak a language
A language without words
See my body says a lot of things and can be used as a weapon
A weapon to tease or to please or just to say how much I care
Damn, my body
There are no words about it
That's my body

Bitter

They say I'm bitter
And I need to
Move on
I say I'm horny
And can't let
Go of the DI
To have a touch
That makes everything
So right and special
Something that makes
You want to melt
Just in the first thought of foreplay
Ladies you know what I mean
When it's just right
And fits you just right
And then it walks a way
With the owner
See baby
It's not the man we want
It's what's in his pants
We can get over the
Heart break and not being together
But the kisses
NO NO
The back pain and the hot
Passionate nights
NO NO
So don't think it's you
It's just what you got
That makes it HARD
To let go... (Smile)

I woke up this morning

I woke up this morning
Legs wide open on the bed
Rubbing my thighs
Feeling an itch between my lips
That's placed between my thighs
I wanted a touch
A kiss
A squeeze
Anything to make this itch go away
As I moaned into my pillow
I could feel these juicy lips/tongue
In between my legs licking my click
I could feel the juices rolling down the backs of my thighs
Just as the sucking and licking got intense
I feel it stop
As another pleasure enters in between by legs
I feel this thick long pleasurable stick
Enter into my walls
With deep penetration the moaning from my mouth
Gets louder and louder
Screams are flowing as this feeling goes deeper and deeper into me
But it stops again
As I feel my body being flipped over
And body arched up
As this big thick long thing enters me again
But this time from the backside
Noise levels rise
As the movement of my hips rise and become more engaged
The feeling is making each part of my body explode
As the feeling stops again
But this time ending with a mess on my sheets
I woke up this morning!!!

The End

I don't know where this road is going to take me. But I hope on a journey of life. People say we all go through life and at one point will be heart broken. It's just a part of life and this is all a part of me. A story told with such energy and power that it can't help but to touch your soul.

The end, this is the ending of a time in my life when love was there and lost. I will always love my first love. But there are other stories out there I need to write.

I fell in love with music.....

The End

.

www.ingramcontent.com/pod-product-compliance
Lightning Source LLC
Chambersburg PA
CBHW062026040426
42447CB00010B/2160